FINALLY FREE

Three Lessons in the Parable of the Prodigal Son

BRYAN WOLFMUELLER

CONCORDIA PUBLISHING HOUSE · SAINT LOUIS

Published by Concordia Publishing House
3558 S. Jefferson Ave., St. Louis, MO 63118-3968
1-800-325-3040 • cph.org

Manufactured in the United States of America

---

1 2 3 4 5 6 7 8 9 10 34 33 32 31 30 29 28 27 26 25

Index of Artists

The name in parentheses is the more common name than Ruskin uses (or is an alternative spelling of the name).

Finally Free Endorsements

Pastor Wolfmueller is a remarkable pastoral theologian. I always chuckle when I'm in some backwater locale around the globe and someone approaches me with this question, often heavily accented by the speaker's mother tongue: "You know Worldwide Wolfmueller?" Ha! YES! The remarkable clarity of the Gospel, which animates all Pastor W's work, shines even more brightly in this little gem of a book. "He welcomes sinners and eats with them," the religious experts complained of Jesus. This book takes a wondrous look at the third and often ignored character in Jesus' parable of the prodigal: the disgruntled brother. Pastor W speaks to the Pharisee in every one of us and drives us to repentance, forgiveness in Jesus, and joy in living forgiven as we encounter our neighbors.

—Pastor Matthew C. Harrison, LCMS president

Bryan Wolfmueller is well known for his ability to break down abstract biblical ideas into life-changing spiritual truths. He does it again in this beautiful book by employing insights from Lutheran theology (especially Law and Gospel) and highlighting three slaveries that threaten us and three freedoms lavishly given to us by God through Christ Jesus. This is a perfect study for individuals or groups. Highly recommended!

—Reed Lessing, The Edwin F. and Esther L. Laatsch Chair of Old Testament Studies, Concordia University, St. Paul

Bryan Wolfmueller offers a careful and contextual study of a well-known parable and shows how the heavenly Father would tear down walls both of guilt and of pride, which separate us from divine love. The Father's love extends both to the guilt-ridden and self-righteous among us. Highly recommended!

—Rev. Dr. Mark Brighton, emeritus professor of biblical languages and literature, Concordia University Irvine

Wolfmueller has done it again! With pastoral clarity and theological grit, *Finally Free* names the real enemies—living for your appetites, despairing in your guilt, and trusting in your own righteousness—and dismantles them with the Word of Christ. This isn't shallow self-help or flimsy moralism; it's the death of the old Adam—of fleshly indulgence, despair, and pride. But it is also the resurrection of the new man in Baptism. For the weary, the guilty, and the self-righteous alike, this book delivers what only the Gospel can: You do not belong to your sin, your guilt, or your works—you belong to Christ. You are a redeemed child of God.

—Rev. Dr. Matthew Richard, pastor of St. Paul's Lutheran Church, Minot, North Dakota, and author of *Will the Real Church Please Stand Up? Seven False Churches*

CONTENTS

A Note About Scripture Translation

All Scripture passages are the author's translation. They are mostly modernized adaptations of the King James Version, with reference to the original languages.

Introduction

This little book is about the parable of the prodigal son. In that beautiful story, Jesus outlines the three slaveries threatening us and the three freedoms He wants to give us.

Writing a book about such a famous, familiar, and beloved passage of Scripture is a dangerous proposition. How many joyful tears have been shed on that passage in the Bible, where prodigal sinners see themselves embraced in the merciful arms of their gracious heavenly Father? How many sermons have used this text to open heaven and the very heart of God to timid souls afraid that they have "sinned too much" and "gone too far"? There is a risk that any unfolding of this parable would dull the splendor of the Gospel so gloriously held forth by our Lord.

My hope is the opposite. I hope that another look at the parable will add to the wisdom and comfort the Lord wants to give us. Particularly, I'd like to focus on the older brother, who is sulking in the field. When we think of the parable of the prodigal son, we almost forget that there are two sons and that the second son is the entire point of the parable. Will he join the feast?

I'd like to offer two pieces of evidence for this argument.

First, the parable of the prodigal son is the third in a series of three lost-and-found parables in Luke 15. We'll look more closely at this later, but for now, notice that the first two parables are much more straightforward and direct.

A shepherd is in the wilderness with one hundred sheep. One wanders off and is lost. The shepherd searches for the lost sheep, finds it, and has a party with his friends and neighbors to celebrate the sheep's return. Jesus concludes, "I say to you, that likewise, joy shall be in heaven over one sinner who repents, more over ninety-nine righteous persons who need no repentance" (v. 7).

A woman has ten pieces of silver. One is lost, and she searches into the night to find it. When she finally finds the missing coin, she calls together her friends and neighbors to celebrate that she has found the coin. Jesus concludes this parable, "Likewise, I say to you, there is joy in the presence of the angels of God over one sinner who repents" (v. 10).

Lost. Found. Joy.

But the third parable, the parable of the prodigal son, adds the element of the older son. We don't know what the ninety-nine never-lost sheep think about the one who wandered off. There is no concern for the nine silver coins, which were always where they were supposed to be. However, mention of this older brother, offended by his father's joyful generosity and standing alone in the field, is a detail that is both unique and essential to this third parable.

Second, remember the context of all three parables:

> Then drew near to [Jesus] all the tax collectors and sinners to hear Him. And the Pharisees and scribes murmured, saying, "This man receives sinners and eats with them." (vv. 1–2)

In these three parables, Jesus addresses the murmuring scribes and the grumbling Pharisees. They are offended that Jesus ate with sinners, talked with tax collectors, forgave the sins of the worst kinds of people, and welcomed the worst into the kingdom of God. The scribes and Pharisees are offended by God's mercy. They are the older brother standing in the field refusing to join the party, incredulous that the father would kill the fatted calf for his wayward, wasteful, sinful, irresponsible, lazy, and wicked brother.

That's the point. Jesus is after the scribes and Pharisees. He is exposing their bad doctrine and false theology.

He presents their theological errors about God, the Law, righteousness, and eternal life. He demonstrates how flawed and misleading their thinking and teachings are.

The scribes and Pharisees are all about the Law. They arrange their lives in such a way so that they can claim to keep the Law and the commands of God. Their hope is in their obedience. They stand in contrast to Jesus' teaching of God's grace and mercy. Because of this, the scribes and Pharisees are the bad guys in the Gospels, serving as the foil to Jesus' teaching.

However, and we must not miss this, Jesus loves the scribes and Pharisees. Jesus also died for the scribes and Pharisees. Jesus' mercy extends to the scribes and Pharisees.

When Jesus, in this parable, is exposing their joyless refusal to join the celebration of God's grace, He does so because He wants these scribes and Pharisees to participate in this joy, to be part of the kingdom of God.

I often hear preaching about how Jesus loves the sinners and the outcasts, but He blasts away at the religious rulers. "Jesus loves the sinners and despises the self-righteous religious people." No. Jesus loves the scribes and Pharisees. He loves the self-righteous. Jesus shed His blood for sinners who don't even know they've sinned.

He is the Savior for people who have no idea they need saving. The father loves the older brother sulking in the field and wants him to share in the joyful feast. Jesus is not content for the scribes and Pharisees to stand there grumbling while He eats with these sinners. He wants them to sit down and join the meal.

Jesus' desire for all to join Him is essential for us.

We each have a sinful flesh that would love to wander from the Father's house and do whatever we want.

We each have a troubled conscience that wonders if we've sinned too much to be welcomed back into the Father's care.

And we each have a little Pharisee living in our hearts. We consider ourselves to be good and righteous based on our own efforts.

Each of these three inclinations is a form of slavery. Each is illustrated in this parable. And our dear Lord Jesus desires to set us free from each of them.

CHAPTER 1

Belly Slaves

Father, give me the portion of the goods that falls to me. (Luke 15:12)

Jesus introduces us to the youngest son in the middle of his rebellion. He goes to his father and asks for his inheritance.

What an insult. The son is saying, "I wish you were dead. The inheritance is more valuable to me than you are." Why? We can discern some of his motivations from the actions that follow.

"And not many days after, the younger son gathered all together, and took his journey into a far country, and there wasted his substance with riotous living" (v. 13).

The younger son is tired of his father, the family farm, the early mornings, the curfew, the discipline, the rules, the work, and the requirements of his father. He feels hemmed in, bound up, and constrained by his father. He feels enslaved.

He's not. This is *not* the first slavery; the father's house is not a prison, but the devil will tempt us to feel this way. Leaving the father's house is going to feel like freedom. Rebellion, at first, tastes like emancipation.

Imagine this younger son with new sandals, a trimmed beard, a wallet full of money, and an imagination full of exotic towns—and the exotic women who inhabit those towns. Imagine the smile on his face as he steps through the gate, off his father's farm, and breathes in his new life. Let's stop the action and pretend we've met this younger son there and talk to him.

"You look happy!"

"For the first time in my life!" he says, buoyantly.

"What's going on?" we ask.

"The old man's given me my inheritance. I don't belong to him anymore. No more up with the roosters. No more lunch in the fields. No more 'early to bed, early to rise' nonsense. I can finally do what I want and live life on my terms. I'm finally free."

"Where are you going?"

"Don't know."

But we know. We know where this road ends. We know that it wanders through bars and beds, loneliness amid crowds, and longing that is somehow never satisfied until there is no more money, no more "friends," and then nothing but a truly empty stomach groaning to eat with the pigs.

The first slavery is belly slavery—slavery to our appetites and passions.

"And when he had spent all, a mighty famine arose in that land, and he began to be in want. And he went and joined himself to a citizen of that country, and he sent him into the fields to feed the swine. And he longed to fill his belly with the husks that the pigs ate, but no one gave him anything" (vv. 14–16).

The journey that started when he stepped off his father's farm ends here in a stranger's field. That bright, burning lust ends in grime. That hunt for pleasure turns up empty. It always does. Hunger and lust are never satisfied.

This is not a uniquely Christian insight. Almost all philosophers recognize that you cannot give free rein to your lusts; you cannot simply run after pleasure. Hedonism ends in disaster. The laws set by temporal authorities, culture, and self-discipline must restrain our desires. But the fire of lust burns hot, and our sinful flesh is bent on rebellion.

Paul describes it this way: "Their end is destruction, their god is their belly, and they glory in their shame, their mind is on earthly things" (Philippians 3:19). Their god is their belly; they are serving their corrupt desires; they are slaves to their lust.

However, note carefully that this slavery initially appears to be freedom.

"While they promise themselves freedom, they themselves are the slaves of corruption: for by whom a man is overcome, by the same he is brought into bondage" (2 Peter 2:19).

What a perfect verse to capture this paradox. Slavery to the corruption of our sinful flesh is accomplished under the banner of liberation and the self-promise of freedom.

The younger son had no idea he was leaving freedom for slavery. He thought the very opposite. He thought he was escaping the tyranny of his overbearing father to be free to do what he thought was best. This trick is as old as the world. It reminds us of how the devil tempts Eve (see Genesis 3:1–6).

"Did God really say that you are not supposed to eat from every tree in the garden?"

"We may eat," Eve responds, "of the fruit of the trees of the garden, but of the fruit of the tree which is in the midst of the garden, God has said, 'You shall not eat of it, neither shall you touch it, lest you die.'"

"You will not surely die." Here, we carefully note the devil's argument. "*God knows* that in the day you eat, your eyes will be opened, and you will be like God, knowing good and evil."

"God knows." The devil is not too concerned about what Eve thinks about the fruit. Instead, the devil is concerned about how Eve is thinking about God, or better, what Eve thinks God is thinking about her.

"God knows that you won't die. God knows that the fruit is good. In fact, God knows that the fruit will make you like Him, and that's why He has forbidden you from eating it. He's holding something back from you. He's keeping you down. His rules are for Him, not for you. He does not have your best interests in mind. And if you are going to be truly free, you have to break through the slavery of His restrictions."

The devil convinced Eve and Adam and continues to try to convince all of their children that the Law of God is what enslaves us. To be free to live how we want to live, to do what we want to do, to chase after our desires, to give free rein to our sinful flesh—this is the slavery that the devil offers as freedom.

It's an astonishingly simple argument that happens repeatedly in our conscience.

"You want to do that thing?" the devil asks.

"Yeah."

"I want you to do it too. We're on the same team. But you know who doesn't want you to do it?"

"God."

"Yup. He's against you. He doesn't want you to be happy." Whatever. Whatever.

It's a foolish argument with an incorrect and blasphemous conclusion, but it's very seductive to us sinners who "want to do that thing."

Let me illustrate how this slavery works. Imagine you're walking through some frontier town in the Old West. You walk past the jail, and sitting there, behind bars, is the devil.

"What are you doing out there?" he asks.

"What do you mean? I'm walking along the street, headed toward the general store," you respond.

"Oh," he says, "I see. You think you're free out there."

"Yes," you respond, confused. "I'm free out here, and you are in jail."

"You've got it all wrong," he argues. "Freedom is in here. In here, we do whatever we want. Out there are laws and rules, and the sheriff is breathing down your neck.

Do this. Don't do that. In here, there are no rules. We do what we want. We are truly free."

To prove his point, he takes a shot of whiskey and kicks the person next to him in the shins.

"That looks like fun," you say as you walk into the cell.

"And not many days after, the younger son gathered all together, and took his journey into a far country, and there wasted his substance with riotous living" (Luke 15:13).

I am a belly slave, and I live in the midst of belly slaves.

Belly slavery is not only an individual problem. Entire cultures can be enslaved to their passions and deceived by the faux freedom of libertinism. The classic name for this is *hedonism*. Hedonism claims pleasure is the highest good and the pursuit of pleasure is the best life. We live in a hedonistic time, in a hedonistic culture.

Oh, the irony. Culture is usually a prohibitive force—something to fill in the gaps between what is illegal and what is wrong. It might not be unlawful to talk rudely to a stranger, but it would be wrong, and the culture sets those norms in place. It might not be illegal for a young dating couple to lie down together and act as though they are married, but it would be wrong, and the culture establishes those norms. Culture should have names for these wrong activities and insults for the people who participate in them. Culture, functioning properly, is fighting against our sinful instincts and corrupt desires.

Culture forbids. At least it is supposed to.

But like the younger son in the parable, this anti-flesh pressure of the culture feels like bondage. *Repressive* is the word we use to diminish and reject it. Our culture has been engineered to work in the opposite direction. Instead of repressing our lusts, it accelerates them. "Pursue your desires." "Chase your pleasures." "Don't let anyone tell you what you want is wrong." The prohibitive work of culture is turned on its head and now gives momentum to our pursuit of pleasure.

This might seem new to us, like something that's never happened in history, but there is nothing new under the sun. Chasing pleasure (or avoiding pain) is a hedonistic form of Epicureanism. Epicurus was an ancient Greek philosopher who taught the ideal of avoiding pain (which he mainly taught came from the idea that the gods interfere with us, both in this life and after this life). For Epicurus, a practical atheism is the best way to live. Some of his followers quickly flipped the switch from avoiding pain to pursuing pleasure. This is the hedonistic approach to life, and it has the power to capture (and destroy) cultures.

Hedonism has become a significant aspect of our modern culture. The illusion of sin as freedom has almost a mythic force in our imagination. It is the driving force of the sexual revolution and the transgender revolution. The Ten Commandments are considered irrelevant, and Christian freedom is labeled "repressive."

There is power in seeing the truth and recognizing the slavery hiding behind the sin.

First, for our sanctification. We can recognize the power of sin at work in us. We recognize the devil's lying voice when he puts forth the choice to sin as an act of freedom.

Second, this understanding of the nature of temptation helps Christians explain to others how their minds and hearts work. The Christian, as a student of the human conscience, often knows more about a person than that person knows about him- or herself, and this is one of those places. "The Lord is not the bad guy. He wants what is good for you, even if it doesn't seem like it. Your wants are often wrong."

Third, as the argument of Christianity pushes against the argument of a hedonistic culture, this warning about the bondage of sin is essential to articulating a joyful Christian worldview.

Recognizing it is one thing, but how is one freed from belly slavery? The first step is recognition, seeing the lie. To wake up and realize that chasing your passions feeds your belly and indulges your lust is, in fact, enslavement. Jesus says it like this: "Whoever commits a sin is a slave to sin" (John 8:34). When we recognize our passions as sinful, our actions as wrong, our motivations as selfish, our intentions as empty, and our life of belly slavery as an empty offense, then we have come to ourselves, and we are ready for the first freedom: contrition.

The Half Freedom of Contrition

"And when he came to himself, he said, 'How many hired servants of my father's have bread enough, and to spare'" (Luke 15:17).

The first slavery, belly slavery, gives way to the first freedom: contrition. The prodigal son realizes he is lost, hungry, empty, and enslaved. He realizes that he has done wrong and has offended God and his father.

We hear him crafting his confession in verse 18: "I will arise and go to my father, and will say to him, 'Father, I have sinned against heaven, and before you.'"

Contrition is the recognition that you are a sinner. There is a word we don't like to hear: *sin*. We can admit that we make mistakes; "to err is human." We can acknowledge that we're not blameless; "nobody's perfect." But to admit that we are sinners, lawbreakers, and God-offenders is difficult.

Why? Why is contrition so difficult?

THERE IS A STANDARD
CREATED BY GOD
THAT APPLIES TO ME
THAT MATTERS, AND
I HAVEN'T KEPT IT.

Each part of that sentence is difficult for us. We don't want standards. If there are standards, we want to create them ourselves. If God made them, we want them to apply to other people. If they apply to us, we don't want it to matter. And, at last, if these meaningful, God-created standards do matter, we want to keep the standard and remain right according to these rules.

But if, against all our protesting, there is a standard created by God that applies to us that matters and that we haven't kept, then we are, in fact, sinners: guilty before God and man.

Just as sin at first appears to be freedom, contrition at first seems like slavery, defeat, or surrender. Contrition is indeed a loss. It undermines the argument of our self-righteousness. (There will be much more on this in the discussion of the third slavery.) Contrition involves admitting our weakness of mind, heart, and strength. We fail to know, want, will, and do the right thing.

The freedom of contrition can take a few different forms.

"I am not who I want to be." Regret.

"I am not who the people I love (or respect or want to impress) want me to be." Shame.

"I am not who God wants me to be." Guilt.

What we are aiming for is a profound spiritual knowledge of our sin. We want to see that our weakness and brokenness are far greater than we can imagine. It is a spiritual death. And even more than that. When combined with the fear of God, or even the recognition of God's holiness, this contrition is terror—the recognition that we are appalling to God, offensive to His holiness, and undeserving of His love. We rightly deserve His punishment here in time and forever after death.

This conclusion is so deep that only the Holy Spirit can bring us to this (see John 16:8–9).

Often, the depth of this realization is not reached. We recognize that we are sick but not dead, guilty but not worthy of condemnation, broken but not offensive to God's holiness.

For now, let's consider the baseline natural contrition, the simple recognition that our lusts are never satisfied, chasing pleasure is an empty pursuit, our wills are weak, our wants are confused, and God is probably a little disappointed with us.

In this state of half contrition, we try to fix ourselves. Like Adam and Eve, we sew fig leaves together to cover our shame and imagine it works. This is the religious impulse of humanity. I can make up for my failures by doing the right thing. The old theologians referred to this as the *opinio legis*, the "opinion of the law," the inherent theological logic of our sinful flesh that suggests, "If my wrongdoing is the problem, my well-doing is the solution."

We are in debt to God's goodness, but we can work our way out of it.

This is where many people will move from Epicureanism to Stoicism, from pursuing pleasure to pursuing virtue, from an easy to a meaningful life. Rather than avoiding all suffering, they understand that life is more; we are made for more than being stuffed full of whatever we want. Rather, meaning is found in being poured out.

The shift is seen around *discipline*. Is that a good or bad word? For the belly slave, *discipline* is always bad. For the contrite, discipline is (difficult and painful and) good.

To be emancipated from belly slavery is to move into a different kind of life. I no longer wander around looking for something to consume and trying to avoid being consumed. I am now concerned with right and wrong, truth and lies, good and evil. I recognize that there is a God and that He is big, good, and probably mad—mad at me for being bad and playing a part in desecrating His good creation.

With this new life comes an entirely new set of dangers and an almost immediate temptation to another slavery. For this reason, we should consider *contrition* only as half freedom. It is only the first half of enlightenment.

Listen to the way it works with the prodigal son.

"I will arise and go to my father, and will say to him, 'Father, I have sinned against heaven, and before you. I am no longer worthy to be called your son. Make me as one of your hired servants'" (vv. 18–19).

Contrition gives way to despair, to the slavery of unworthiness. If belly slavery is trying to end the groan of the stomach, despair is trying to find a balm for the groaning conscience. It is the religious impulse of humanity. We will turn our attention to this enslavement in the next chapter.

CHAPTER 2

Despair

I am no longer worthy to be called your son. (Luke 15:19)

The prodigal son moves from one slavery to another. He is a hungry, pig-feeding slave in a strange land, but he works it out in his head that his father's slaves have it better than this. He will go back to the farm—not as a son but as a slave. His father will be his master.

"Father, I have sinned against heaven, and before you. I am no longer worthy to be called your son. Make me as one of your hired servants" (Luke 15:18–19). The Greek word *doulos*, the normal Greek word for "servant" or "slave," is not used here. The word *misthios*, "a hired hand," is used instead. The slaves lived on the farm and were given shelter, food, and education for their children. They were an integral part of the household. The hired hands were not. They were even less. They would arrive in the morning, work alongside the slaves, receive their wages, and leave.

When the prodigal son imagines asking to become a hired hand, he is saying, "I know I'm not worthy to be your son, to live in your house, to have a place under your roof or at your table. I'm not part of the family, nor am I part of the home. I'll get here early. I'll work all day. You won't have to take care of me at night. You won't hear me complain. I'll work hard, and I'll make up for all that I've lost."

The second slavery is despair.

Despair knows its unworthiness. Despair knows its sins.

Despair knows that it has offended the father and lost its place in the family.

Despair is worried about the father's anger, about the consequences of failure. Still, despair also feels trapped, with nowhere to go.

But strangely, despair makes us think we must solve the problem, fix the situation, and make amends for the damage we have caused. Despair results in a theology of works.

"I'll be a great slave, a hardworking slave; I'll fix what I've broken; I'll make up for my mistakes." It's an impossible promise, as if this prodigal son's work could somehow replace the inheritance that he squandered, as if the fig leaves could really cover shame, as if our half-hearted volleys at goodness could earn everlasting life. But that doesn't stop us from trying.

Despair is a theological slavery. That is, it has to do with how we think about God and ourselves. The theology is simple: I am bad; God is mad; I suppose I'd better get busy.

Three Groans

Three deep and painful groans arise from the human condition. The first is the belly: hunger, thirst, lust, desire. Belly slavery is motivated to stop this groan, to ease this pain, to scratch this itch, to be appeased. Pleasure, we think, will end this groan. It does not.

The second groan is the groan of the conscience. It is the groan that knows that something is wrong in the world, that something (or everything) is broken, and that we have something to do with that. It is the groan that the prodigal son feels in the gutter. He is hungry, sure. But he is guilty. He is wrong. He is bad. He is broken. He is undeserving. The prodigal son uses the word that best captures this groan: *unworthy.*

The third groan we'll mention in passing: the groan of loneliness, or the need to see and be seen, to hear and be heard. There is a deep, built-in need for connection—a longing for companionship and conversation—but that is a topic for another time.

The prodigal son has moved from addressing the first groan to addressing the second groan. He realizes that the eyes, the belly, and the fallen flesh will never be satisfied and that chasing that satisfaction is a vain pursuit. The pain of his desires is eclipsed by the pain of guilt, shame, regret, and unworthiness.

But just like before, when he went chasing his lusts to fix the belly groan, he now comes to us with a plan to address the conscience groan: "I'll fix the problem. I'll go to work. I'll make up for all the things I've done wrong. I was a rebellious child, but I'll be a faithful servant. I'll dig my way out of this hole in my heart." He's given up on freedom; he'll be a servant.

We're All Servants, This Is True

Despair is the engine that drives most of the world's religions, the hidden motivation of most good works. God is good and big and mad, and I'm scrambling to avoid His anger with my accomplishments. What other choice do I have?

It is from the groaning conscience that the religious impulse of humanity arises. Like belly slavery, the slavery of despair is also more than an individual phenomenon. All of the major religions, worldviews, and ideologies of the world are addressing this conscience groan, this awareness that something is wrong out there and in here.

Francis Pieper, an early teacher and professor in The Lutheran Church—Missouri Synod, famously said that there are only two religions in the world: the religion of the Law and the religion of the Gospel.

> How many essentially different religions are there in the world? . . . There are not a thousand, not even four, but only two essentially different religions: the religion of the Law, that is, the endeavor to reconcile God through man's own works, and the religion of the Gospel, that is, faith in the Lord Jesus Christ, belief wrought through the Gospel by the Holy Ghost that we have a gracious God through the reconciliation already effected by Christ, and not because of our own works. (*Christian Dogmatics* 1:9–10)

We are talking about this first religion—the religion of the Law, the religion of works, the religion built to take away the conscience's groan by our own works and efforts, the religion of despair. "I'm not worthy to be your son," this religion says. "Make me one of your hired servants."

We are sympathetic to this condition. We also find ourselves burdened with guilt and shame. When we are set free from the slavery to our bellies, we recognize that we are lawbreakers living out of order with God's design. We see that we are sinners, that we are truly unworthy. The words of the old liturgical confession of sins express it best:

> I, a poor, miserable sinner, confess unto Thee all my sins and iniquities with which I have ever offended Thee and justly deserved Thy temporal and eternal punishment. (*The Lutheran Hymnal*, p. 16)

What are we to do? We join the prodigal son on his slow walk home barefoot, hungry, plodding, and plotting. "Maybe, just maybe, my father will let me try, will let me work, will let me serve." We rehearse our confession, plan our service, and worry about what will happen if we manage to pull it off. We have a sinking feeling that we won't. And then, the second freedom arrives.

The Freedom of Faith, Which Is the Freedom of Grace

Imagine the prodigal son arriving back at his father's farm, standing there at the gate. The last time he was here, he couldn't wait to leave; he never looked back to see the father standing there watching, praying for his son's return. He was a belly slave full of lust and greed. But now he stands, trembling, humbled, wondering what will happen. What will his father do when he sees him? Will he look him in the eyes, or will he look away? Will he spit in his face, tell the servants to beat him and throw him out, or put him in prison? That's what he deserves, but he has no choice.

He steps through the gate, repeating his confession under his breath: "Father, I'm not worthy to be called your son. Make me one of your hired servants." He shuffles forward. "Father, I'm not worthy to be called your son. Make me one of your hired servants." He sees the outline of his old house; his heart skips a beat. He is afraid. "Father, I am no longer worthy to be called your son. Make me as one of your hired servants." People are noticing him. Workers in the field recognize him as he gets closer, and they begin to whisper to themselves. He's shaking. "Father, I am no longer worthy." And then it happens; he sees his father. For just a moment before his father sees him, he almost gives up, turns, and runs away. But before the despair gets complete control, the father turns to see his son, and without hesitation, he leaps up, grabs his robes, and starts to run down the dusty path toward his son.

The son is frozen, standing there. “What’s happening? Why is he running to me? Is he going to tackle me? Beat me? His face doesn’t look angry. There are tears! But he is smiling and running full speed right at me. What do I do?” He starts his confession. “Father, I am no longer worthy to be called your son.” But before he can get another word out, the father takes him up in his arms and kisses his face, his tears splashing on his cheeks. He lifts the son off the ground and holds him to himself. He is not angry with him; he delights in him.

“Quick,” he cries to the servants, “the robes, the good ones. The ring, shoes, the fatted calf. This is what I’ve been waiting for, praying for, planning for all along. This—my son—was lost and is found.”

The words “my son” ring in our ears. Those astonishing words of grace and mercy and the forgiveness of sins stand in contradiction to all our plotting and planning to make up for our sins, to pay back our transgressions. Those two words set us free from the slavery of despair.

"Make me as one of Your hired servants."

God won't have it. He won't hear of it. He wants sons, not slaves. "Therefore you are no longer a slave but a son" (Galatians 4:7).

Freedom from despair comes by the grace of God, from the promise of the Gospel, and from the forgiveness of our sins.

The father holds nothing against the son. His rebellion is put away, his sin is forgiven, his shame is covered, and his failure is forgotten. He is restored. This is the business of the ring and the robe, the shoes and the fatted calf; the son is brought back into the family.

All of this comes at a price. Half of the inheritance is still lost, and now more is being spent. But it is the father who pays the price for the son's failings. This parable happens in the shadow of the cross of Jesus. Jesus did not deserve His suffering. He is the innocent one who was punished for crimes that He did not commit. He is the perfect one who was condemned for the sins of others. God the Father made Christ, who knew no sin, to be sin for us, that we might become the righteousness of God in Him (see 2 Corinthians 5:21).

The old theologians called this doctrine the *vicarious satisfaction.*

Vicarious because Jesus took the place of sinners. Think of the scapegoat in the Old Testament (and all the sacrifices with blood in the Old Testament). The high priest would place his hands on the head of the goat and confess the sins of Israel, and then that goat would be led out into the wilderness to die. The goat didn't do anything wrong, but it carried away the sins of others. Jesus is that scapegoat. John the Baptist preaches, "Behold, the Lamb of God, who takes away the sin of the world!" (John 1:29). He claims and carries sins that are not His. (This is how we should hear the preaching of all the Old Testament sacrifices. When we see the bull or goat or lamb sacrificed, we see that God graciously accepts the death of another in our place.) Jesus took your sins, all that you've done wrong, and suffered for them in your place.

This is the business of the cross and the true suffering of Jesus. When we reflect on the suffering of the cross, we often think of the physical pain, the lash of the whip, the sting of the thorns, the piercing of the nails, and the torture of crucifixion, but this is only a small part of the suffering. We sometimes think of the shame of the cross, the spit on His face, the stripping, the wagging fingers of the crowd: "He saved others, let Him save Himself. He said God loved Him, let God deliver Him now." This, also, is only part of the suffering. The deep affliction of the cross comes not from Pilate or the Jews or the soldiers but from God Himself. "My God, My God, why have You forsaken Me?" (Matthew 27:46). Christ Jesus endured what we deserve and suffered for what we are due. Because of our sins, He was forsaken so that we might be forgiven and accepted. God's righteous wrath was poured out on Christ.

There is wrath to be spent, a cost to sin. This is the doctrine of the atonement. Forgiveness is not a decision. It is a sacrifice. God is truly offended by our sins and rightly angry at our rebellion, but that offense was put on Christ. On the cross, Jesus put Himself between us and the wrath of God, and in His suffering and death, God's anger was put away. Our Lord Jesus took our place, suffering what we deserve, paying the price for our sins, so that we might be eternally with Him in the fellowship of God and enjoy eternal life.

All of this is to say that when the father runs down the path and scoops up his prodigal son, there is a price to be paid. He doesn't just forget the son's sins; he pays for them, suffers for those sins himself, and bears up the shame of his son. There is always suffering in forgiveness. The father endures what the son deserves.

Dear reader, dear friend, this is what the Lord has done for you. Your sins are forgiven. You are set free from the slavery of despair. Your plans to fix your problems and make up for all your sins were never going to work anyway. The cross of Jesus is God picking up His robes, running down the path, wrapping His arms around you, and calling you His child. Despair no more. "Behold what manner of love the Father has given to us, that we should be called the children of God!" (1 John 3:1).

Emancipation Proclamation

We need to consider briefly how this freedom gets to us. God accomplishes our salvation through the death of Jesus on the cross. He brings that salvation to us through the preaching of the Gospel.

All His saving gifts come to us in a word, specifically, in a promise. God gives us His saving grace as good news. Salvation does not come to us by drinking some magic potion, eating some secret food, swimming in some mystical pool, or having an ecstatic vision. No, salvation comes to us in the preaching and the hearing of the word of promise. "It has pleased God by the foolishness of the preaching to save those who believe" (1 Corinthians 1:21). "Faith comes by hearing, and hearing by the word of God" (Romans 10:17). God speaks salvation.

There are two general ways that the Lord speaks to us. First, He instructs and commands. This is the teaching of the Law in which God tells us His will for our lives. We keep the Law by obedience, by doing what is commanded of us. Second, God gives us blessings and makes promises. We keep a promise by believing it.

A command is not given to be believed but followed. "Touch your toes." "I believe you." Believe what? There was no promise, only an instruction.

On the other hand, it is also ridiculous to make a promise. "I'll be home at 6:00 p.m." And you bend over to touch your toes?! No, a promise is kept by believing, by faith.

When the Bible tells us that we are saved by grace through faith, it means that our salvation comes to us through a word of promise (not a command) and that we keep that promise by faith (not by works and obedience).

The Gospel is the specific promise of the forgiveness of sins and eternal life through the suffering, death, and resurrection of our Lord Jesus Christ. Faith in Christ is believing and trusting in that promise, building our hope on His pledge of forgiveness, salvation, and eternal life.

Faith, then, is the second freedom, but not faith floating around as some abstract faithiness. Saving faith is our confidence in the promise of God, our being grabbed up by the running father and brought into the home, our being clothed with the righteousness of Christ, our hearts washed with His blood, our sins claimed by Christ so that God's wrath is His and His life is ours.

Faith is freedom from despair, from the hopeless hoping in ourselves, from the emptiness of our attempts to clean our conscience by bathing in dirt. Faith trusts the promise and rejoices in this eternal truth: Christ died for sinners.

The Two Parts of Repentance, Which Are the First Two Freedoms

Taken together, the first two freedoms are the two parts of repentance.

We often hear repentance as the changed life that follows faith in Christ. This is not repentance but the fruit of repentance. Repentance is the heart changed by the preaching of God's Word.

The Holy Spirit brings us the Law of God to show us that we are sinners, that we have offended God. The result is the first (half) freedom: contrition.

The Holy Spirit brings us the Gospel to show us Christ, the Savior of sinners, and promises the forgiveness of all our sins. The result is the second freedom: faith.

The Augsburg Confession, presented in 1530 to show what Lutherans teach, defines repentance this way:

> Now, strictly speaking, repentance consists of two parts. One part is contrition,

> that is, terrors striking the conscience through the knowledge of sin. The other part is faith, which is born of the Gospel or the Absolution and believes that for Christ's sake, sins are forgiven. It comforts the conscience and delivers it from terror. Then good works are bound to follow, which are the fruit of repentance. (Augsburg Confession, Article 12, paragraphs 3–6)

Repentance is freedom, a double freedom from sin and despair. Repentance is the confidence that I cannot save myself and that God in Christ has saved and delivered me. Repentance is God rescuing us from the slavery to our belly and our guilt. Repentance is the staggering prodigal son come home, scooped up into the Father's arms, sinners rejoicing in the Lord's mercy, forgiveness, and life that never lacks or ends. God be praised!

But the parable of the prodigal son does not end with the joyful graciousness of the father to his prodigal son. The older brother is out in the field, and it turns out that he is also enslaved and needs to be set free. We'll turn our attention to him in the next chapter.

CHAPTER 3

PRIDE

THESE MANY YEARS I SERVED YOU. (LUKE 15:29)

Remember that the parable of the prodigal son is the last in a series of three parables in Luke 15, and up to this point, each parable has followed a similar pattern:

- The shepherd searched for the lost sheep, found it, and rejoiced with his friends. "I say to you, joy like this will be in heaven over one sinner who repents, more than over ninety-nine righteous people who need no repentance" (v. 7).
- The widow searched for her lost silver coin, found it, and rejoiced with her friends. "Likewise, I say to you, there is joy in the presence of the angels of God over one sinner who repents" (v. 10).
- The prodigal son, left with his inheritance, wasted everything and limped back home. The father sees him, runs to him, embraces and restores him, and prepares a feast to make merry and rejoice.

We expect the punchline next. Jesus should say something like, "There is overflowing rejoicing before the throne of God over one sinner who repents." Instead, Jesus tells us, "Now his elder son was in the field" (v. 25). The story is not over, and this last part of the parable, it turns out, is the point.

This older son represents the grumbling Pharisees. "This man receives sinners and eats with them" (v. 2). They were angry that Jesus associated with sinners. They were offended that Jesus ate with tax collectors. They were troubled by Jesus' teaching about mercy. They refused to share in the joy of repentance.

Pride is the third slavery and the most difficult of all to overcome. You can hear it in what the older son says to his father. "Look, these many years I served you, and I never transgressed your commandment, but you never gave me a goat that I might make merry with my friends, but as soon as this, your son, has come, who devoured your property with prostitutes, you killed for him the fatted calf" (vv. 29–30).

"I did everything you asked. I worked hard. I kept the rules. All these years, I," wait for it, "served you." There it is. The older son does not think of himself as a son but as a servant. He has no father, only a master. His life has been all rules and rewards.

Both boys think of themselves as servants. The difference? The older boy is the good servant, the obedient worker, the one the father should be proud of. He is waiting for his reward. After all, he has earned it. "Surely," he thinks, "Father loves me even more because I'm not like my brother. I'm no thief or prodigal."

"I'm a Good Person."

We are all hardwired to think of ourselves as good.

Most people will admit that they are not perfect, that they've made mistakes; "to err is human," after all. However, we've convinced ourselves that the mistakes we've made were unavoidable and insignificant and were probably made with good intentions. We are experts in arguing the case for our goodness.

Imagine your conscience as a little internal courtroom, and your life is on trial. Whenever you do something wrong or foolish, your conscience takes it as an accusation. You feel guilty, but you immediately begin to make your case. "You were tired. No one was hurt. They deserved it. You meant well. Next time will be different." We are all defense attorneys defending ourselves, asserting our righteousness, and excusing our sins. Sometimes we even succeed, convincing ourselves of our innocence and pronouncing the verdict, "I'm a good person."

(As an interesting aside, we often take other people to court in our conscience. If we like them, we will frequently excuse their sins. If we don't, we become their accuser and judge, making the case against them.)

It seems like this is what was happening with the older son as he worked the fields. He was thinking of his hard work, his obedience, and how he followed his father's rules. "I'm doing what I'm supposed to do. I'm living right." He also likely thought of his brother. "How could he? He's wasted everything. He's broken every commandment. He's ruined everything." The verdict: "I'm a faithful servant. I deserve something good. He's a faithless fool. He deserves nothing but punishment."

Of Pride

Pride is delicate.

Pride is easily offended. Pride judges.

Pride is angry.

Pride is self-centered. "I am the hero of this story. But not in a fun way. I'm the hero who constantly must fend off other heroes to keep other people from becoming too important."

Pride is selfish.

Pride is discontent.

Pride loathes itself. It hates the work it does to make the case for its goodness. The older son didn't like working in the field; he never liked working in the field. He only did it because he was supposed to, or because it was the way to win his father's approval, or perhaps because he thought he would get something out of it. Maybe he thought he would inherit the farm and rule it like a tyrant.

Pride is transactional. And it always thinks it is getting the short end of the stick.

Pride is jealous.

Pride is joyless.

Pride is ugly.

The scribes and Pharisees were proud, convinced that they were holy and ready to see God. They looked down on sinners. They despised the unclean. The scribes and Pharisees were self-righteous, self-important, self-declared judges of goodness and truth. The scribes and Pharisees were set apart for God. They were held in bondage to this pride. It distorted their view of themselves, others, and God. Pride is a damning false comfort.

It stands in the way of the humility of contrition and the confidence of faith. These Pharisees were in great danger of missing the kingdom of God.

Jesus Also Loves the Scribes and Pharisees

It is common in Christian preaching to point out how much Jesus loved the tax collectors and sinners but despised and rebuked the scribes and Pharisees and "religious people." But can we not see that Jesus also loved the scribes and Pharisees? Jesus also died for the religious people. Jesus also suffered for the theological pride of the self-righteous. Jesus is after the scribes and Pharisees, these grumbling, complaining, holier-than-thou scribes and Pharisees. He looks upon them in love. He sees all the sin that they can't see, all the self-delusion, animosity, anger, and despising of sinners, all masquerading as holiness. He sees all the greed, lust, lies, shame, and the thankless, joyless ideas of God, all covered over with the adornment of piety. Jesus sees that they have no room for mercy, yet He still shows them mercy.

The parable of the prodigal son is a picture of that mercy. To understand this parable, we must see these words as an expression of Jesus' love and compassion for the scribes and Pharisees. He is calling them out of the slavery of pride and into the freedom of joy. He is giving this parable with the intent that they will repent of their pride and rejoice in the Father's mercy.

Jesus is after them.

He wants them to know the Father's joy, the freedom of forgiveness, and the life that He came to bring to all mankind. The joy of the Father is not only for the sinful prodigal son but also for those enslaved in self-righteousness.

But the prison of pride and the slavery of self-righteousness are tremendous obstacles to overcome. Jesus goes hard after the scribes and Pharisees, the whitewashed tombs, the brood of vipers, and the hypocrites, not because He hates or despises them but because He loves them. The hard preaching of the Law is a hammer to break their stony hearts before it is too late.

It is impossible to have the Lord's verdict of mercy if we are declaring ourselves innocent and holy.

The scribes and Pharisees will either have a broken, contrite, repentant, and humble heart and come into the Kingdom, or they will have a heart of stone that is crushed and demolished on Judgment Day. Jesus hammers away, pounding the chains of pride that bind them to their self-righteousness. He exposes their hypocrisy in the hopes of covering their sin with His kindness. He invites them into the fellowship of the joy and peace of God's overwhelming mercy.

Preaching "Son" to Slaves

The final scene of the parable is the conversation of the gracious father with his obstinate older son, who is standing in the field, refusing to come to the feast.

> And [the older brother] was angry and would not go in. Therefore, his father came out and entreated him. And he, answering, said to his father, "Look, these many years I served you, and I never transgressed your commandment, but you never gave me a goat that I might make merry with my friends, but as soon as this, your son, has come, who devoured your property with prostitutes, you killed for him the fatted calf." And he said to him, "Son, you are ever with me, and all that I have is yours. It was right that we should make merry and be glad, for this your brother was dead and

> is alive again; and was lost, and is found."
> (vv. 28–32)

The first word of the father says it all: "Son." "You are not my servant; you, also, are my son. Everything that is mine is yours. You haven't earned it or deserved it; you've inherited it." Jesus presses that word up against the scribes and Pharisees and their legalism: *son*. This one word contains all of the Law and the Gospel. It is a rebuke of humanity's religious delusions, encompassing all of our attempts to achieve an acceptable holiness on our own terms, including our legalism, self-righteousness, self-appointed rituals of righteousness, and our tendency to judge ourselves as holy and others as unclean. All of it, says Jesus, is a vain and puffed-up slavery that wants to earn what God would freely give. Pride is a double sin. It insults God, as it wants to earn what God wants to give. "Son, all that I have is yours." "Son" is a call to repentance from the slavery of pride.

"Son" is also a word of comfort, a preaching of peace. "You are not my servant; you are my son," the father says graciously to the older son. It is a call to rejoice in the gifts, to be part of the feast, to come into the home. "All your attempts to win my affection have not succeeded, but neither have they failed. They were unnecessary in the first place. You have always been a beloved son, and you have always had a gracious father."

That father's grace is far beyond what you knew, what you imagined, what you expected, and even what you wanted.

Here we get to the crux of the slavery of pride: It is offended at the mercy of God. It sees the feast fixed up for the prodigal son and scoffs. "That's not right. Look at all I've done right, and I get nothing. Look at all he did wrong, and he gets everything."

Pride is a twofold slavery. On the one hand, I'm convinced of my own goodness and glory. On the other hand, I'm convinced that other people are corrupt and evil. I deserve heaven; they deserve condemnation. I've passed; they've failed.

Pride wants to be judged according to all it has done.

Pride wants others to be judged on what they have not done.

Pride wants Law, all Law, with no Gospel.

Pride wants Jesus off the cross, the blood unspilled, mercy recalled, because whatever

it is that God is doing there is not necessary or desired.

It should be the prodigal son who is slaughtered, pride thinks, not the fatted calf.

But God is a God of mercy. There is forgiveness with Him; therefore, He is feared. He will have compassion on whom He will have compassion, and we can't stop Him. He will love and forgive and serve and deliver and cleanse us of all unrighteousness. He will be the Savior of sinners, the Redeemer of rebels, the Hope of lawbreakers, the Joy of the world.

The Third Freedom: Joy in the Lord's Mercy for Others

The third freedom, the freedom from the slavery of pride, is found in God's mercy to others. The third freedom is the freedom of joy, particularly joy in God's mercy and love for other people.

This is the angels' joy.

Angel Joy

The three lost-and-found parables in Luke 15 are all about joy, but we should note carefully who is joyful. We don't know if the sheep is joyful about being rescued in the wilderness, but we are told that the shepherd, "when he has found it, he lays it on his shoulders, *rejoicing*. And when he comes home, he calls together his friends and neighbors, saying to them, '*Rejoice with me*; for I have found my sheep which was lost'" (vv. 5–6, emphasis added).

Again, we don't know how the silver coin felt about being found and rescued from the dusty corner, but we know how the woman felt: "When she has found it, she calls her friends and her neighbors together, saying, 'Rejoice with me; for I have found the piece which I had lost'" (v. 9).

It is not the joy of the thing or person that is found that Jesus mentions, but the joy of the finder and the joy of their friends.

This is the joy of heaven, the joy of the angels. "I say to you, that likewise, joy shall be in heaven over one sinner that repents, more over ninety-nine righteous persons who need no repentance" (v. 7). "Likewise, I say to you, there is joy in the presence of the angels of God over one sinner who repents" (v. 10). "It was right that we should make merry and be glad, for this your brother was dead and is alive again; and was lost, and is found" (v. 32).

The angels rejoice over a salvation that was not for them.

The angels cannot be saved. But the angels rejoice in a salvation that is not their own. They rejoice in the repentance of sinners, the forgiveness of sins, and the kindness and mercy of God, which is not for them but for us.

The angels are not the object of the Lord's saving work but the observers. They watch and wonder while rejoicing that God is good and kind to undeserving creatures.

The parables call us into this joy. We are the lost sheep, yes, but we are also the shepherd's friends. We are the lost coin; this is true, but we are also the woman's neighbors. We are the prodigal son, but we are also the older brother, and the joy into which we are invited is not only the joy of our salvation but the joy of other people's salvation, the joy of the Lord's saving work for the entire world.

And we can be even more specific. We are all tempted to have a list of people we don't want Jesus to die for. Maybe there are names on that list of people who have abused and hurt us. Maybe there are broad categories on that list, mostly the evil people or the people who have not tried as hard as we have. You can't take that list to the party with you. The third freedom is joy in God's love for people you do not love.

Something Different Is Happening in the Courtroom of the Conscience

Remember how we all have this courtroom in our conscience where we are (mostly) accusing others and excusing ourselves. The third freedom makes something different happen in our consciences.

Let's use an Old Testament picture to describe it. When the Lord brought Moses and all the people out of slavery in Egypt, He led them to Mount Sinai. There, He gave Moses instructions for building the tabernacle as the place of true worship. This was a tent with two rooms. The outer room, known as the Holy Place, featured a table for the showbread, a lampstand, and a small incense altar. The priests would minister daily in the Holy Place. There was a second room, the Most Holy Place, which held the ark of the covenant, a gold-plated box that held the Ten Commandments, Aaron's rod, and a jar of manna. The top of this box was made of gold and was called the mercy seat. It was God's throne.

The high priest only entered the Most Holy Place once a year, on the Day of Atonement. The high priest would offer special sacrifices (a bull for the sins of the priest, a goat for the sins of all the people) and carry the blood into the Most Holy Place, placing it on the mercy seat.

We can see the preaching: The blood of the sacrifice covers over the guilt of the law. The blood of the sacrifice makes the Lord's throne a *mercy* seat, not a *judgment* seat.

In this ritual, the Lord painted a picture of what was to happen centuries later. Christ, our High Priest, offered Himself as the sacrifice for our sins. When He ascended to the right hand of the Father, He brought His blood into the heavenly Most Holy Place as evidence of His all-sufficient sacrifice. In the heavenly courtroom, the evidence is admitted and the verdict is spoken: Our sins are forgiven. We are righteous.

> For Christ has not entered into the holy places made with hands, which are the figures of the true; but into heaven itself, now to appear in the presence of God for us. (Hebrews 9:24)
>
> But this man, after He had offered one sacrifice for sins forever, sat down on the right hand of God. (Hebrews 10:12)

The blood of Jesus interrupts God's righteous judgment. Now heaven is full of rejoicing. This interruption is brought down to us in the preaching of the Gospel.

Through the Word of God, the Holy Spirit stands up in our conscience. It interrupts the proceedings, the accusations, and the excuses. The accusation of the Law mutes all defense based on our own righteousness, and we become truly guilty before God. (This is the first half freedom of contrition.) Then sounds forth the sweet heavenly verdict: By the suffering and blood of Jesus, your sins are forgiven. (This is the second freedom of faith.) Now, all the arguments against my neighbor, all my holding on to their sins, are let go. These, also, are forgiven. (This is the third freedom.)

As We Forgive Those Who Trespass Against Us

Jesus illustrates this with the parable of the unforgiving servant. This parable teaches us what it means to pray, "Forgive us our trespasses as we forgive those who trespass against us." The parable is in Matthew 18:23–35.

There was a king who had a number of debtors. One in particular had an enormous debt: ten thousand talents. A talent was equivalent to one year's wages. This man is called to appear before the king, and the debt is demanded of him. He can't pay, so he begs for mercy and more time. "Lord, have patience with me, and I will pay it all" (v. 26).

Note that the king hears this request but doesn't answer it. He doesn't give him more time. He does more: He forgives the entire debt. "The lord of that servant was moved with compassion, set him free, and forgave him the debt" (v. 27). Amazing. That massive debt went somewhere; someone had to pay it. We see that the king was willing to suffer that loss instead of his servant. This is a picture of the cross of Christ, where the innocent Son of God suffered the guilt of sinners. This is the first scandal of the parable, the overwhelming grace and mercy of the king in forgiving such a debt.

Then, there is a second scandal. The servant whose debt is forgiven leaves the king's presence, but then the forgiven servant sees another servant who owes him money—one hundred denarii (a denarius was one day's wage). He grabs him by the throat and demands the money. This servant prays the exact words that were just prayed to the king: "Have patience with me, and I will pay it all" (v. 29). But the servant whose tremendous debt was just forgiven by the king has no mercy on his fellow servant and has him thrown in prison.

It is shocking to hear that this man, freshly forgiven for an unpayable debt, is unable to be generous with his fellow servant. The king is shocked too. He hears about it and is overflowing with wrath and indignation. He calls the first servant back and reinstates the debt and the punishment.

To see what is going on, I'd like to go back and adjust the parable. Let's pretend that instead of forgiving the debt, the king heard the request for more time and granted it. "Please give me more time." "Okay, you have three months to pay back your debt, and if you fail, I will throw you and your family in prison." What would happen? This servant would leave the king's presence and go looking for everyone who owed him anything. He would wring their necks and demand their payments. If there was no forgiveness, then this would be the right thing to do. He would be a debt collector for the king, and the king would commend him, "Well done. You have paid me everything you owed me." This would be the normal thing to do if there was no forgiveness.

Indeed, the servant is acting as if his debt is not forgiven. He is going about his normal business of debt collecting as if there was no mercy, no grace, no forgiveness, no canceling of his debt.

It may seem right that we hold people accountable for their sins. Indeed, there is an essential place for justice, and this is why the Lord has instituted local, state, and federal governments, among other institutions. But we cannot act as if there is no forgiveness of sins, as if our tremendous debt to God's holiness has not been paid by the death of Jesus on the cross. We are forgiven, and that changes everything. Mercy is how God acts toward us, and mercy is becoming the way we act toward one another.

Out in the Field

The parable of the prodigal son ends with the words of the father to his older son: "It was right that we should make merry and be glad, for this your brother was dead, and is alive again; and was lost, and is found" (Luke 15:32). There they are: father and son, standing in the field.

That's it. The parable is over. We don't know what happened—whether the son came into the feast or stayed in the field—and that is the point. Jesus puts the scribes and Pharisees listening to the parable at this crossroads.

It is the warmth and joy of the Father's feast, or it is the outer darkness of the field.

Remain in the field, in the slavery of pride and joyless bondage of your self-righteousness, or come into the house, join the feast, look at the face of your younger brother, smile, and rejoice that he is back, alive, forgiven, and home. Eat and drink and sing and dance and share in the generosity and grace of the Father and recognize that the mercy of the Father toward your younger brother is the same mercy that He has for you.

Conclusion: The Joy of the Angels

It was right that we should make merry and be glad. (Luke 15:32)

Remember where we started:

We each have a sinful flesh that would love to wander from the Father's house and do whatever we want.

We each have a troubled conscience that wonders if we've sinned too much to be welcomed back into the Father's care.

And we each have a little Pharisee living in our hearts. We consider ourselves to be good and righteous based on our own efforts.

Each of these three inclinations is a form of slavery. Each one is illustrated in this parable.

Our dear Lord Jesus comes to set us free.

If the Son sets us free, we are free indeed (see John 8:36).

Where are you in the parable of the prodigal son? Somewhere on the devolving path to belly slavery? Slumped over and shuffling, enslaved to despair? Standing in the field, indignant, self-righteous, a slave to pride?

It probably depends on the day. We are all inclined to all three slaveries. Our sinful flesh is bent toward bondage. Some days, we will find ourselves chasing after our lust and desires. Some days, we will find ourselves wallowing in guilt. Some days, we will find ourselves looking down our noses at everyone else. Some days, we will manage to do all three before breakfast. Jesus has come to set us free from these slaveries.

> You are all sons of God through faith in Jesus Christ. (Galatians 3:26)
>
> Therefore you are no longer a slave but a son, and if a son, then an heir of God through Christ. (Galatians 4:7)
>
> Stand fast therefore in the liberty in which Christ has made us free, and do not be entangled again with a yoke of bondage. (Galatians 5:1)

The wisdom of God's Law shows us our sins, brings us to ourselves, and gives us the first half freedom of contrition.

God's Gospel promises us forgiveness of all sins. It assures us of God's kindness, tender mercy, and love through the suffering, death, and resurrection of our Savior, Jesus Christ, which gives us the second great freedom: faith.

The overflowing mercy of God for the world gives us the third freedom: humble joy. The Lord saves others and gathers us with them in His feast of new life.

Our heavenly Father wants sons, not slaves. He has adopted you into His holy family, made you His heir, given you His name, and given you a seat at the table of His mercy and kindness, which He gives to all sinners.

> Behold what manner of love the Father has given unto us, that we should be called the children of God! (1 John 3:1)